Futility & Sacrifice

The Canadians on the Somme, 1916

by

N.M. Christie

The Access to History Series
Number 2

CEF BOOKS
2004

"Access to History; The Canadian History Series:
Number 2"
Futility and Sacrifice: The Canadians on the Somme, 1916
ISBN 1-896979-08-4

Published by: CEF BOOKS
                  P.O. 29123
                  3500 Fallowfield Road
                  Nepean, Ontario, K2J 4A9.

Editor-in-Chief: R.B. McClean

Access to History; The Canadian History Series

Acknowledgements:
We would like to thank the Royal Canadian Legion Ontario Command branches for the support that made this book possible.

This book is dedicated to the memory of the Canadians who willingly gave their lives in the defence of freedom in the Twentieth Century.
Lest We Forget.

Maps by Constable Enterprises, Stittsville, Ontario.
Graphics and Layout by Imágenes Graphic Arts, Ottawa, Ontario.

Front cover: *The Battle of Courcelette* by L.A. Weirter (1873-1932) (CWM 8931)

Printed in Canada

Table of Contents

EUROPE 1914-1918

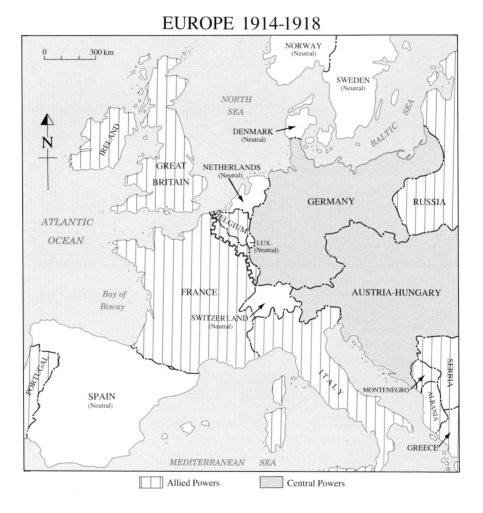

0   300 km

NORWAY
(Neutral)

SWEDEN
(Neutral)

NORTH
SEA

BALTIC SEA

DENMARK
(Neutral)

IRELAND

GREAT
BRITAIN

NETHERLANDS
(Neutral)

GERMANY

RUSSIA

N

ATLANTIC
OCEAN

BELGIUM

LUX.
(Neutral)

Bay of
Biscay

FRANCE

AUSTRIA-HUNGARY

SWITZERLAND
(Neutral)

PORTUGAL

SPAIN
(Neutral)

ITALY

MONTENEGRO

SERBIA

ALBANIA

GREECE

MEDITERRANEAN   SEA

☐☐☐ Allied Powers   Central Powers

iv

Introduction

1916 was the year of "blood." It was the start of the war of attrition, of endless slaughter, that epitomized the First World War. In the two major battles that were fought in 1916, at Verdun and the Somme, more than 2,200,000 soldiers of all nationalities were killed, wounded or listed as missing.

The Battle of the Somme was the first major British offensive of the war. It was Britain's chance to teach the Germans that it was unwise to challenge the mighty British Empire. In theory, the British attack at the Somme was to be a simple matter of marching over the German positions and continuing the advance all the way to Berlin. The initial breakthrough would be achieved by shelling the extensive German trench systems into oblivion. 120,000 enthusiastic British troops, including 790 Newfoundlanders, would then walk through the shattered German defences virtually unscathed.

The plan failed and on the first day of battle, July 1st, 1916, 20,000 British soldiers died for minimal gain. A further 40,000 were wounded or became prisoners. In one fell swoop, Kitchener's volunteers had been smashed and the worst day in the history of the British Army was recorded. In the days and weeks that followed, the British used massive artillery barrages to attack heavily defended German trenches. They captured some, only to lose many to German counter-attacks. By the end of the battle, the British Army, including South Africans, New Zealanders, Australians, Newfoundlanders and Canadians, had suffered roughly 420,000 casualties.

The Canadians arrived on the Somme in September 1916 when the battle was two months old. They relieved the Australians near Pozieres. What they witnessed was a pock-marked landscape like that of the moon; villages were obliterated and rotting corpses were strewn everywhere. At Pozieres, 23,000 Australians had lost their lives, been wounded or had gone missing.

On September 15th, 1916, the Canadians attacked as part of a major offensive that used tanks for the first time in war. Over the next two months, Canadian troops assaulted the German positions at Courcelette known as Regina Trench, Hessian Trench and Desire Trench. Often they charged against uncut barbed-wire and were always confronted by the inevitable German counter-attacks. More than 24,000 Canadians were killed, wounded or listed as missing in the battles of the Somme. Today, behind the peaceful facade of the meandering Somme River, a countryside known for its rolling fields, fishing and tranquillity, are the terrible scars of that war now embodied in some 400 military cemeteries. Imagining the hell that was the Somme in 1916 is impossible for us. The only evidence today of the ferocity of the Somme battles is the harvest of steel from the farmers' fields. After 80 years, rusted shell fragments, thousands of shrapnel balls, bullets, buttons, grenades and bones still surface. Otherwise, the once infamous names of the muted victories of 1916, the Sugar Refinery, Courcelette, Regina Trench, Kenora Trench and the Quadrilateral, are forgotten.

More than 8,000 Canadians paid with their lives for those futile victories and their legacy, our heritage, deserves to be remembered. It is their legacy, their contribution to Canada, and the contribution of thousands of others just like them to whom this book is dedicated. Our knowledge of what they did and what they fought for keeps them alive in our memory.

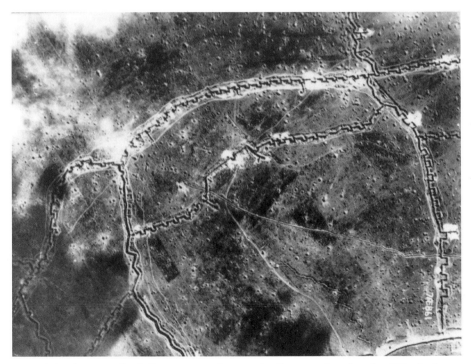

Aerial photograph of German trenches on the Somme showing Stuff Redoubt.
(PAC C43989)

GENERAL TRENCH-LINE
ON THE WESTERN FRONT
1914-1918

COMPONENTS OF THE CANADIAN CORPS
The Somme: 1916

1ST CANADIAN DIVISION

1ST INFANTRY BRIGADE	2ND INFANTRY BRIGADE	3RD INFANTRY BRIGADE
1ST BATTALION (WESTERN ONTARIO)	5TH BATTALION (SASKATCHEWAN)	13TH BATTALION (BLACK WATCH OF MONTREAL)
2ND BATTALION (EASTERN ONTARIO)	7TH BATTALION (BRITISH COLUMBIA)	14TH BATTALION (ROYAL MONTREAL REGIMENT)
3RD BATTALION (TORONTO REGIMENT)	8TH BATTALION (90TH RIFLES OF WINNIPEG)	15TH BATTALION (48TH HIGHLANDERS OF TORONTO)
4TH BATTALION (CENTRAL ONTARIO)	10TH BATTALION (ALBERTA)	16TH BATTALION (CANADIAN SCOTTISH)

2ND CANADIAN DIVISION

4TH INFANTRY BRIGADE	5TH INFANTRY BRIGADE	6TH INFANTRY BRIGADE
18TH BATTALION (WESTERN ONTARIO)	22ND BATTALION (CANADIEN-FRANCAIS)	27TH BATTALION (CITY OF WINNIPEG)
19TH BATTALION (CENTRAL ONTARIO)	24TH BATTALION (VICTORIA RIFLES OF MONTREAL)	28TH BATTALION (SASKATCHEWAN)
20TH BATTALION (CENTRAL ONTARIO)	25TH BATTALION (NOVA SCOTIA)	29TH BATTALION (BRITISH COLUMBIA)
21ST BATTALION (EASTERN ONTARIO)	26TH BATTALION (NEW BRUNSWICK)	31ST BATTALION (ALBERTA)

3RD CANADIAN DIVISION

7TH INFANTRY BRIGADE	8TH INFANTRY BRIGADE	9TH INFANTRY BRIGADE
ROYAL CANADIAN REGIMENT *(NOVA SCOTIA)*	1ST CANADIAN MOUNTED RIFLES *(SASKATCHEWAN)*	43RD BATTALION *(CAMERON HIGHLANDERS OF WINNIPEG)*
PRINCESS PATRICIA'S CANADIAN LIGHT INFANTRY *(EASTERN ONTARIO)*	2ND CANADIAN MOUNTED RIFLES *(BRITISH COLUMBIA)*	52ND BATTALION *(NEW ONTARIO)*
42ND BATTALION *(BLACK WATCH OF MONTREAL)*	4TH CANADIAN MOUNTED RIFLES *(CENTRAL ONTARIO)*	58TH BATTALION *(CENTRAL ONTARIO)*
49TH BATTALION *(ALBERTA)*	5TH CANADIAN MOUNTED RIFLES *(QUEBEC)*	60TH BATTALION *(QUEBEC)*

4TH CANADIAN DIVISION

10TH INFANTRY BRIGADE	11TH INFANTRY BRIGADE	12TH INFANTRY BRIGADE
44TH BATTALION *(MANITOBA)*	54TH BATTALION *(BRITISH COLUMBIA)*	38TH BATTALION *(EASTERN ONTARIO)*
46TH BATTALION *(SASKATCHEWAN)*	75TH BATTALION *(MISSISSAUGA HORSE)*	72ND BATTALION *(SEAFORTH HIGHLANDERS OF VANCOUVER)*
47TH BATTALION *(BRITISH COLUMBIA)*	87TH BATTALION *(GRENADIER GUARDS OF MONTREAL)*	78TH BATTALION *(WINNIPEG GRENADIERS)*
50TH BATTALION *(ALBERTA)*	102ND BATTALION *(NORTH BRITISH COLUMBIA)*	73RD BATTALION *(BLACK WATCH OF MONTREAL)*

The Make-up of an Army

The Army - The British Forces on the Western Front were divided into four or five Armies. The British Army in the field was commanded by Field Marshall Sir Douglas Haig. Throughout the war the British Army varied in strength, but usually employed 4,000,000 (1917) soldiers in the field. The Canadian Corps belonged to the 1st British Army, but had stints with the 4th Army as well.

The Army Corps - An Army Corps consisted of a number of Infantry Divisions, depending on its needs. The Corps was commanded by a Lieutenant-General. Its numeric strength varied, but could put as many as 120,000 men in the field. The Canadian Corps was made-up of four Divisions, all Canadian, but often had British Divisions attached for special attacks or battles.

The Division - The Infantry Division was composed of three Infantry Brigades and had 20,000 soldiers. It was commanded by a Major-General. The make-up of the 20,000 soldiers included 12,000 infantry, 3,500 artillerymen, 750 in a medical section, and 2,000 engineers and pioneers.

The Brigade - The Infantry Brigade was commanded by a Brigadier-General and consisted of four Battalions (4,000 infantrymen). Each Brigade had engineers, signals, a field ambulance, trench mortar unit and machine-gun unit.

The Battalion - The Infantry Battalion consisted of 1,000 men. This was the theoretical strength of the unit; after headquarters staff, illness, wounded, etc. were deducted, a Battalion would normally put 650 rifles into the line. It was commanded by a Lieutenant-Colonel. Each Battalion was made-up of four companies (200 men), commanded by a Major or Captain. In turn, the company was broken into four platoons commanded by a Lieutenant and each platoon into four sections commanded by a Sergeant.

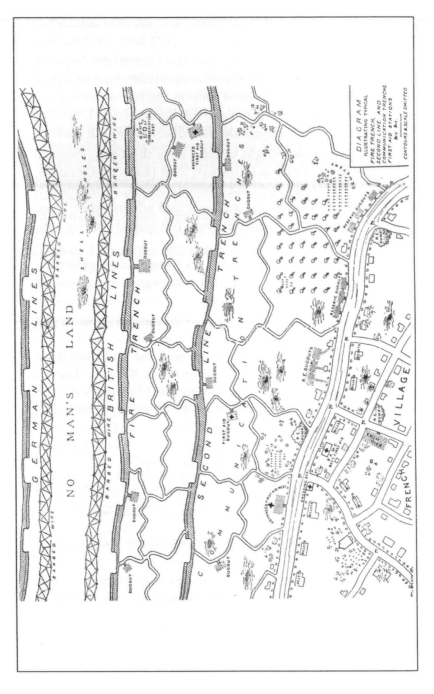

Schematic of a Trench System, 1916

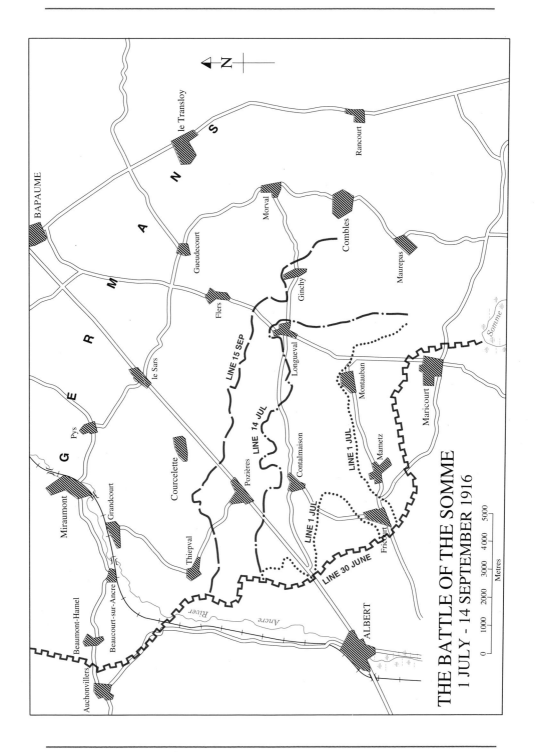

THE BATTLE OF THE SOMME
1 JULY - 14 SEPTEMBER 1916

BAPAUME

le Transloy

G E R M A N S

Rancourt

Gueudecourt

Morval

Combles

Maurepas

Flers

Ginchy

le Sars

LINE 15 SEP

Longueval

Montauban

Maricourt

Pys

LINE 14 JUL

Courcelette

Pozières

Contalmaison

LINE 1 JUL

Mametz

Miraumont

Grandcourt

Thiepval

LINE 1 JUL

Fricourt

LINE 30 JUNE

Beaumont-Hamel

Beaucourt-sur-Ancre

River Ancre

ALBERT

Auchonvillers

Somme

N

0   1000   2000   3000   4000   5000

Metres

THE BATTLE OF THE SOMME

July to November, 1916

Historical Overview

The Battle of the Somme opened on July 1st, 1916, with a massive British attack launched over a 28 kilometre front. Ushered in with a week-long artillery bombardment which fired 1.5 million shells into the German positions, the attacking British divisions expected the July offensive to be successful. They were on the way to Berlin!

Their plan was to bombard the German trenches with a ferocity previously unseen in warfare. For seven days, they would pulverize the German positions. The shelling would cut the barbed-wire entanglements, collapse the dug-outs and kill the occupants. Then the soldiers, heavily-laden with 30 kilograms of equipment, would climb out of their trenches, walk to the German lines and capture the few survivors. In a similar manner, they would continue on and take the next line of trenches and then breakthrough into the open countryside. It was simple British ingenuity. The fact the French had tried the same thing in 1915, and failed, did not bother the British Generals.

But the strategy of a massive artillery barrage, followed by a general assault across No Man's Land, failed. On July 1st alone, the British Army suffered 60,000 casualties, including 20,000 dead. The shock of this failure rocked the British public. Many of the soldiers killed came from the same towns, lived on the same streets, worked together and belonged to the same clubs and churches. As a result, the losses of that one day of battle profoundly affected the British people.

Those killed were not all British. The Newfoundland Regiment was the only non-British battalion that attacked on July 1st. In 45 minutes, 272 Newfoundlanders were killed and 438 were wounded. They were not even in the main attack; they did not even enter the German trenches! Little Newfoundland, Britain's oldest colony, was devastated by that single day of terrible carnage.

1

How could they have faltered so badly? They failed because the Germans had tunnelled into the chalky Somme farmland, building dugouts 20 to 30 metres deep. They were too well protected to be affected by any artillery barrage. The bombardment had also failed to cut the barbed-wire entanglements protecting the approaches to the trenches. Consequently, at 7:30 a.m. on the July 1st, 1916, when the bombardment ended and the British troops climbed out of their trenches, the Germans came out of the well-protected dugouts, placed their machine-guns on the parapet of the trench and mowed down the attackers. The firing was so intense the German machine-guns over-heated. The slaughter was enormous. In the complete confusion that followed, several attacks were made when a breakthrough was thought to have been achieved. It was because of one of these ill-advised attacks that July 1st became a day of mourning to all Newfoundlanders and Beaumont-Hamel encapsulated a name to be dreaded.

The Newfoundlanders

Newfoundland was Britain's smallest lion when war was declared in 1914. But like all others across the Empire, the call of the Mother Country could not be refused and Newfoundlanders enthusiastically enlisted. Proud of their heritage, which was definitely not Canadian, they formed their own Regiment and served with distinction from 1915 to 1918. They were the only Regiment who earned the King's title of "Royal" during the entire First World War.

The 1st Battalion, The Newfoundland Regiment, served with the British Divisions throughout the war and participated in the Gallipoli fiasco in 1915. They were fortunate to escape the bloody battles against the Turks on the peninsula, and after the campaign ended, came to France virtually intact. In France, the Newfoundlanders' luck ran out and in the battles that followed, they suffered enormous casualties. It seemed each time they were committed, everything went wrong.

Their first battle in France was on July 1st, 1916, at the Somme. The men of the Newfoundland Regiment were not scheduled to be in the first wave of the assault. They were held in reserve, opposite a small French village called Beaumont-Hamel, pending the outcome of the initial attack. Like all the attacks on July 1st, the Generals were confident of success. But the reality was that the opening attack was a complete failure; the storm troops were cut down in front of the German wire with a few survivors actually reaching the enemy's trench-lines. Less than 30 minutes into the assault, it was over and the battlefield was strewn with dead and wounded. The British trenches were full of crippled and dazed soldiers. The shock of their unexpected rebuff threw all into a state of confusion.

Somehow, reports got back that British troops were in the German trenches and needed to be reinforced. At 8:45 a.m., the 1st Newfoundlanders were ordered to attack. The men were in support trenches 250 metres behind the main British line and due to the congestion in the communication trenches could not move forward using the protective trench system. To comply with the order to attack, they would have to cross 250 metres of open land before even reaching the British wire. Loyal to the end, the Newfoundlanders climbed out of their protection and moved towards the main British trench-line and the German trenches beyond.

It was 9:15 a.m.; the attack along the entire front had been smashed and the battlefield was strangely quiet. The only visible movement was the 790 men of the Newfoundland Regiment moving, overland, towards the Germans. The German observers probably could not have believed their eyes. They focussed their artillery and machine-guns on the small band of approaching men and, unleashing a torrent of steel, pulverized them. The fury of the fire must have come like a curtain of death. Soldiers were bowled over by the raining shrapnel explosions; men collapsed as the machine-gun bullets tore through them. The Newfoundlanders were being annihilated. Few even made the British wire and almost none made it to the German lines. In well less than an hour, the pitiful advance had been snuffed out. The battlefield was littered with the dead and wounded of Newfoundland. It was an awful mistake.

"Machine gun fire from our right front was at once opened on us and then artillery fire also. The distance to our objective varied from 650 to 900 yards. The enemy's fire was effective from the outset but the heaviest casualties occurred on passing through the gaps in our front wire where men were mown down in heaps... In spite of losses the survivors steadily advanced until close to the enemy's wire by which time very few remained. A few men are believed to have actually succeeded in throwing bombs into the enemy's trench."

Official War Diary of The Newfoundland Regiment.

The final tally was horrible. Of the 790 Newfoundlanders in the attack, 272 were killed and 438 wounded. Eighty-nine per cent were casualties for no gain. Throughout the small communities across Newfoundland, the telegrams to the unsuspecting families were delivered. It was the same everywhere, whether it was St. John's, Moreton's Harbour, Fogo Bay, Trinity Bay, Channel or Bay Roberts. No family was untouched by the futile slaughter at Beaumont-Hamel. The Ayre family of St. John's lost four members on July 1st. Captain Eric Ayre and two of his cousins, Gerald and Wilfred, died with the Newfoundlanders; his only brother, Bernard, was killed the same day serving with a British Regiment. By the Armistice of 1918, one in four of the 6,000 Newfoundlanders who served in the Great War had died. It was a crushing sacrifice for the small communities of the Island and represented the worst proportionate losses of any of the countries of the British Empire.

FOUR MEMBERS OF ONE FAMILY WHO FELL ON THE FIELD OF HONOUR.
Four members of one Newfoundland family, two brothers and two cousins, fell in France on July 1st, 1916. From left to right they are: Capt. Eric S. Ayre, Newfoundland Regt.; Capt. Bernard P. Ayre, Norfolk Regt.; Sec.-Lieut. Wilfred D. Ayre and Sec.-Lieut. Gerald W. Ayre, both of the Newfoundland Regiment.

"It was a magnificent display of trained and disciplined valour, and its assault only failed of success because dead men can advance no further."
General de Lisle, General Commanding

The failure of the Newfoundlanders on July 1st was not unique. The attack had failed miserably all along the front with the exception of the southern most sector where the German line had been captured. From July onwards, the British attacks would be primarily focussed on driving the Germans back, launching assault after assault against the determined German defenders.

The Battle Rages

Throughout July and August, the Battle of the Somme raged. Attack after attack was delivered; each assault was always preceded by massive artillery bombardments. Small woods and fortified farms became the graves for thousands of soldiers. Usually, the onslaught would bring some territorial gains initially, but always the Germans would counter-attack and would often regain territory that had been lost. The Somme had become a battle of attrition. The price was beyond the General's worst nightmares, but still the attacks were ordered and the men always complied. The only argument the Generals could offer was that Germany, with a smaller population, could not replace the fallen as easily as the Allies. Their original plan of a breakthrough had been forgotten. Surprisingly, the incessant German counter-attacks cost them as many casualties as the British. Both armies were being bled white.

The British forces continued their attempts to push northwards throughout July and August and slowly drove forward against heavy German opposition and numerous counter-attacks. Again, the loss of men and equipment was staggering. British casualties for the months of July (after the July 1st attack) and August were 160,000 men.

Enter the Canadians

Meanwhile, the Canadian Corps, now three Divisions strong, was ordered to the Somme battlefield at the end of August 1916. Boasting a complement of 75,000 men, the 1st, 2nd and 3rd Canadian Infantry Divisions had passed July and August in the always dangerous Ypres Salient. There, in spite of there being no major action, a thousand Canadian lives had been lost. With summer coming to a close, the 1st Canadian Division was moved to the Somme and attached to the II Australian Army Corps. The 2nd and 3rd Canadian Divisions followed in early September.

By the end of August, the fighting to the south of, and along the remnants of the Bapaume-Albert road, had reached the outskirts of Pozieres, a small village that occupied the highest point on the road. Pozieres held a commanding view of the battlefield, and its importance did not go unnoticed by the Germans. They had fought a titanic struggle with the tenacious Australians since late July to maintain their hold on the strategic Pozieres Ridge, but had gradually been forced to give ground. The fighting was so severe in the area around Pozieres that nothing remained of the village and the battlefield was covered with the unburied corpses of Germans and Australians, intermingled, as much of the fighting had been hand-to-hand. Australian forces painfully and expensively drove the Germans from the village, then pushed north and east down the slope of the Ridge towards Mouquet Farm and Courcelette. The eastern drive met determined opposition and yielded little ground. The windmill, on the high point directly east of the village, was captured at the end of August. Australia had paid heavily for its victory at Pozieres. In a little over a month, the Australians had suffered more than 23,000 casualties.

The Pozieres front was still being bitterly contested by both sides when the 1st Canadian Division entered the line on September 2nd/3rd, 1916.

The German Defences

The Somme region of France is beautiful, undulating farmland. The region takes its name from the Somme River, a pretty, meandering stream, that is known for its fishing and wildlife. The actual river is south of where the battle occurred and never became part of it. The main cities of the countryside are connected by arrow-straight Roman roads. A large amount of the fighting took place around the Roman road running along a main ridge connecting the cities of Albert and Bapaume. The countryside is dotted with small French farming villages. In 1916, these villages, such as Thiepval, Mametz, Courcelette and Pozieres, gained infamous reputations. But the villages themselves had long ceased to exist; they had been torn to shreds by the massive military onslaught.

The choice of the Somme as the location from which to launch the first major British offensive of the war is puzzling. It had no particular strategic value and possessed no breakthrough potential. It is an unlikely place to imagine an army could achieve a decisive victory. The question that has perplexed military historians is: why the Somme? Calculating the men lost in this battle, more 1,200,000, only adds emphasis to the debate. There seems to be no answer to this question, other than the Somme was a useful place to launch an attack and start a war of attrition.

As the Somme battlefield lacked any particularly advantageous physical characteristics, the Germans had built a complex series of interconnecting trenches and deep redoubts across the rolling chalk hills.

They took full advantage of every contour. To protect themselves from observation, the Germans generally entrenched on the down side of a slope. The trenches were deep and solid, often strategically interconnected with other switch trenches. A warren of communication and support trenches was utilized for transporting supplies, reinforcements and ammunition. The redoubt positions were often connected by tunnels coming from a variety of places in the support lines. In front of the trenches were dense belts of barbed-wire. Farms had been fortified and linked by a maze of underground works. Each position was designed to extract a great price from any attacker.

"The modern battlefield is like a huge, sleeping machine with innumerable eyes and ears and arms, lying hidden and inactive, ambushed for the one moment on which all depends. Then from some hole in the ground a single red light ascends in fiery prelude. A thousand guns roar out on the instant, and at a touch, driven by innumerable levers, the work of annihilation goes pounding on its way."

Ernst Junger, German Army

The British strategy to capture a trench works was to plaster the German position with high-explosive shells in the hope of collapsing the trench walls, killing or wounding the defenders, and cutting the extensive barbed-wire in front of the trench with shell shrapnel. At the appropriate time, the assault troops would approach the German lines as closely as possible without being hit by their own artillery fire, and at zero hour, rush and take the position. Even if the attack were successful, it did not preclude the Germans digging another trench behind the one just captured or counter-attacking to retake the one lost. In the Battle of the Somme, the Germans did both.

More often than not, the attacks on the strongly fortified German defences on the Somme proved disastrous. The artillery bombardment rarely cut the barbed-wire and the soldiers, trapped in No Man's Land, would be cut down in swathes by the German machine-guns. Sometimes, the Germans allowed the assault troops to enter their front-line trench. Then the German artillery would blast No Man's Land to prevent reinforcements or ammunition from reaching the newly captured position. The reinforcements would be decimated by the German barrage when crossing the open ground and the soldiers in the captured trench would be isolated. At this point, the Germans would counter-attack via

7

Theoretical Front-line Trench, 1916

communication trenches or underground subways. The German stick grenade was the weapon of choice and was a very effective killer with good range and accuracy. These defensive techniques cost the Australians heavily at Pozieres; the Canadians on the Somme learned about these tactics the hard way.

> *"If you want to find the old battalion,*
> *I know where they are, I know where they are,*
> *If you want to find the old battalion,*
> *I know where they are,*
> *They're hanging on the old barbed-wire,*
> *I've seen em, I've seen em,*
> *Hanging on the old barbed-wire."*
>
> *First World War Song.*

The only flaw in the German method was that the counter-attacker often suffered more casualties than the attacker. Germany could not win a war of attrition.

The Canadians arriving at the Somme could not believe the devastation. Even compared to the horrific standards of Ypres, the sights were shocking. It was their first view of total destruction; villages razed, the battlefield a lunar landscape of interconnected shell holes, destroyed trenches, sandbags spread everywhere, old equipment scattered, and thousands of bodies, decomposing in the summer sun. But they did not have much time to mull over these images of immense destruction. They were immediately put in the line in support of the Australians.

> *"Through a gap between two sandbags I was shown the village (Pozieres), where smoke was drifting across skeletons of trees on a torn-up mound. An uneven line of sandbags, stretching across piles of bricks and remnants of houses, faced our way... The ground between our trench and the ruins beyond was merely a stretch of craters and burnt-up grass broken up by tangled wire... The dead were lying in all conceivable attitudes, rotting in the sun... with the heat the smell had become very trying."*
>
> *Paul Maze, French Army attached British Army.*

Despite serving in a secondary role, Canadian losses were considerable. Between September 4th and 7th, the 1st Canadian Division's 16th Battalion (Canadian Scottish) supported the Australian Infantry attack on Mouquet Farm and other German positions north of Pozieres. The

Canadian Artillery in Action by Kenneth Keith Forbes (CWM 8158)

Canadian battalion suffered 349 casualties. On September 9th, the 2nd Battalion (Eastern Ontario) attacked a German trench work south of the Pozieres windmill. The attack was only a local action; one meant to improve the jump-off position for the up-coming major assault.

In this fierce action, Corporal Leo Clarke won the Victoria Cross. Clarke, and a section of bombers, were confronted by 20 Germans. Clarke attacked the attackers, emptied his revolver into them, killed four and captured another. Single-handedly, he had stopped a German attack. Clarke was one of three men from the same street in Winnipeg to win the Victoria Cross in the war. Sadly, two of the three did not survive. Leo Clarke was wounded later in the Battle of the Somme and died of his wounds. He was 24.

The Battle of Flers-Courcelette

The Battle of Flers-Courcelette was the seventh phase of the Battle of the Somme. It was to be a major offensive launched over a 16 kilometre front by 20 British, New Zealander and Canadian Divisions. Roughly 200,000 men were available for the attack. It was to be preceded by a two day barrage, and for the first time in history, tanks were to be used.

The Tanks

The Allied offensives of 1915 had clearly shown that waves of attacking infantry had no chance against modern, defensive weapons. Machine-guns, artillery and entrenched riflemen could stop any assault decisively. The overwhelming superiority of the defence had effectively countered every new offensive tactic that the Generals had created. The result was a stalemate on the Western Front and a war of attrition; it was time to try something different. The industrial revolution had made huge advancements in the technology of metals and machinery and the strategists put the scientists and engineers to work. They were to develop with revolutionary inventions to alter the balance of attack in favour of the offensive.

Many of the inventions were ridiculous and impractical, but important industrial developments brought some fascinating, and deadly, innovations. Amongst the first was the use of poison gas as a weapon. There were improvements in aircraft, flame throwers, and the fabrication of steel

A "tank" winning its way along a Somme village street.

helmets. Tanks were a British invention and were backed by Winston Churchill. They had been in development since 1915 and by September 1916 the first tank, the Mark I, was ready in small quantities. It was decided by the British High Command to use the tanks, piecemeal, in the Battle of Flers-Courcelette. The Mark I was 10 metres long, including a two metre steering tail, weighed 25 tonnes and moved at a maximum speed of six kilometres per hour. That speed was under ideal conditions; on a battlefield, it was reduced to less than one kilometre per hour! They were mechanically fragile and not wholly reliable. Forty-nine of the noisy monsters were allocated for the offensive. Six would attack with the Canadians.

The tanks were brought up secretly and concealed in woods near the front. Allied aircraft flew low altitude flights to cover up the noise of the approaching tanks. At 6:00 a.m., September 15th, 1916, all was ready.

The Plan

Two Canadian Divisions, the 2nd and 3rd, were to participate in the attack. The 2nd Division had the principal role which was to capture the German trenches across the Albert Bapaume road and then push on and take the fortified village of Courcelette just to the north. To achieve these objectives, the 2nd Division deployed five battalions, 4,000 men and the six tanks. Its assault battalions, arranged along the front from east to west, were the 18th (Western Ontario), the 20th (Central Ontario), 21st (Eastern Ontario), 27th (City of Winnipeg) and 28th (Saskatchewan). They were to take the German front lines and advance on the defences in front of Courcelette. A key objective was the fortress known as the Sugar Refinery. Three other battalions of the 2nd Division, the 22nd (Canadien-Francais), 25th (Nova Scotia) and the 26th (New Brunswick), were to follow-up the initial attack and capture Courcelette.

The role of the 3rd Division was to protect the left flank of the 2nd Canadian Division. The 3rd planned to use three battalions in the first attack: the 1st (Saskatchewan); 4th (Central Ontario) and 5th (Quebec) Canadian Mounted Rifle battalions. The 5th CMR was to cover the 2nd Division's left flank and occupy the northern extension of Sugar Trench. The 1st CMR was given the dubious honour of capturing Mouquet Farm, north of Pozieres village. The farm had been a thorn in the side of the Australians. It was heavily defended and linked by a catacomb of underground subways. Several times the Australians thought they had

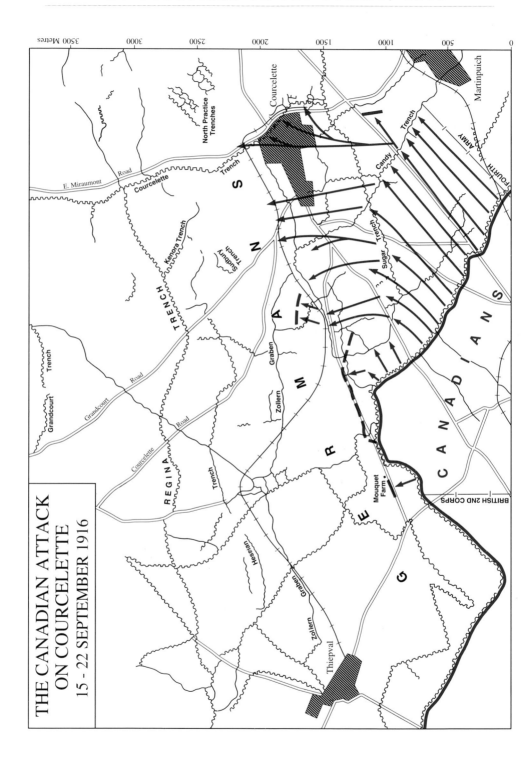

THE CANADIAN ATTACK
ON COURCELETTE
15 - 22 SEPTEMBER 1916

captured Mouquet Farm only to lose it to a German counter-attack which suddenly had popped-up behind them. The 42nd (Black Watch of Montreal), 49th (Edmonton) and Princess Patricia's Canadian Light Infantry (PPCLI) of the 3rd Division were to seize the complex of trenches west of Courcelette village.

For this battle, the Canadians had the distinct advantage of attacking from the heights of Pozieres Ridge. Looking through a trench periscope outwards from the Canadian lines, they could see the chalky spoil from the German trenches and the barbed-wire running across the Albert-Bapaume road. North of the road and just behind the front-lines ran more German trenches, the strong position of the Sugar Refinery and the fortified buildings of Courcelette. In the two kilometres of field running from the village to Mouquet Farm, the chalky spoil, indicating the German trenches, must have appeared like a chessboard to the Canadians. Only two kilometres from the Canadian jump-off point, they could see the outline of Regina Trench snaking across the valley before them. Who could have believed it would take two months and 24,000 casualties for the Canadians to finally reach Regina Trench.

The Battle of Courcelette: September 15th, 1916

At 6:20 a.m., the Canadians attacked. The men of the 2nd Division surged across the 200 metres of No Man's Land and in 15 minutes had captured the German front-line trench. The air was full of machine-gun and rifle fire. German artillery exploded on the Canadian positions. Fighting at the Sugar Refinery was intense, but the soldiers of the 21st Battalion took less than 30 minutes to capture the fortified bastion. The survivors of the initial assault pushed ahead and with the assistance of a heavy artillery barrage entered Candy Trench. Severe hand-to-hand fighting and much close quarters grenade work ultimately secured this important trench-line for the Canadians.

"The air was seething with shells. Immediately above, the atmosphere was cracking with a myriad of machine-gun bullets, startling and disconcerting in the extreme. Bullets from the enemy rifles were whistling and swishing around my ears in hundreds, that to this day I cannot understand how anyone crossed that inferno alive... As I pressed forward with eyes strained, to the extent of being half closed, I expected and almost

Canada's day at Courcelette: furious hand-to-hand fighting in the sugar refinery

felt being shot in the stomach. All around our men were falling, their rifles loosening from their grasp. The wounded, writhing in their agonies, struggled and toppled into shell holes for safety from rifle and machine-gun fire... Rifle fire, however, was taking its toll, and on my front and flanks, soldier after soldier was tumbling to disablement or death, and I expected my turn every moment. The transition from life to death was terribly swift."

Donald Fraser, 31st (Alberta) Battalion.

In the meantime, the 27th and 28th Battalions had overrun strategic Sugar Trench and were advancing towards Courcelette village. German machine-guns, well set-up inside the fortified buildings, spewed death towards the Canadians. Despite the rain of German fire, the men from Canada drove forward and by the end of the morning the success was so great that the follow-up battalions of the 2nd Division were given the task to liberate Courcelette. At 6:00 p.m., the 22nd, 25th and 26th Battalions crossed the fields in front of Courcelette and broke into the village. The fighting was bloody as the Canadians had to capture each farm, each building and each cellar one-by-one. Through great courage, they succeeded, but the village was not completely cleared of German defenders until the next day. Desperate to recapture Courcelette, the enemy launched as many as 14 counter-attacks; however, each was successfully repulsed by the stalwart Canadians.

"If hell is as bad as what I have seen at Courcelette, I would not wish my worst enemy to go there."

T. L. Tremblay, 22nd (Canadien-Francais) Battalion.

The 3rd Division attacks went as well as those of the 2nd Division. The 1st CMR stormed Mouquet Farm and the 5th CMR entered the opposing German front-lines with relative ease. Building on these successes, the 42nd, 49th and PPCLI Battalions had briskly pushed ahead and were fighting for an important German trench known as Fabeck Graben which ran west from Courcelette. Here, the German defences finally stiffened. They were determined not to give an inch and ground lost was swiftly counter-attacked. One of these attacks dislodged the Canadians from their hard-won victory at Mouquet Farm. As night fell, the battlefield quietened and the stretcher bearers came out to clear away the wounded. The field was strewn with Canadian and German dead and the debris of a modern war. However, despite some minor set-backs and the extensive casualties, the first day of battle had been successful for the Canadian Corps.

But what of the tanks? There was no doubt the Germans were surprised by the appearance of the noisy behemoths, but, in the end, unproven technology and little forethought about how to apply these remarkable weapons in warfare undermined their effectiveness. Of the six tanks which

Aerial photograph of Courcelette during the attack, September 15th, 1916.
(PAC 43987)

assisted the Canadian attack, one failed to start and only one really helped in the offensive. Mechanical failure, terrain which the tanks could not negotiate and German shell fire put all six out of action. As a result, the expected success of the "secret weapon" was negligible. Giving away this great secret, without putting it into action after it was thoroughly tested and ready and in the right numbers, certainly was a lost opportunity.

"The noise was deafening... I looked and jumped to my feet but he pulled me down. I saw a great monster coming out of the mist behind us. It was oblong in form... This nose moved up and down as it made its way slowly over shell holes and piles of dirt. Now we could hear the rattle of

machinery that made it go. Then we heard machine-guns firing from its front and side. It dawned on us what it was. The Tanks!"

Archie Gray, Canadian Infantry.

"The great surprise of the attack yesterday was the appearance of Armoured Caterpillars, called "H.M. Land Navy", they can go over any ground, over a 12 foot trench or a 6 foot wall, they knock down anything in front of them... They are very heavy and armed by quick firing guns and manned by the Royal Field Artillery. They carry a search light. Machine-gun fire or a whizz-bang has no effect on them, only a direct hit will put them out and as they are constantly moving, it is difficult to do this... They are the wonder of the war... They are called tanks."

Agar Adamson, Princess Patricia's Canadian Light Infantry.

Over the next few days, the brutal fighting continued in and around Courcelette. The 3rd Division finally captured Fabeck Graben Trench and desperately tried to reach the next major trench system at Zollern Graben, but with little success. Meanwhile, in Courcelette, the 1st Division, which had relieved the 2nd Division, gained an important foothold on the heights just north of the village. As always, however, fierce German counter-attacks made even the smallest gain a costly venture.

Canadian soldiers in action (PAC C46606)

Between September 15th and 22nd, the Canadian offensive at Courcelette incurred 7,230 casualties, but the Canadian Corps had attained its objectives by advancing the front-line by one to one and one-half kilometres.

The Battle of Thiepval Ridge: September 26th, 1916

The General commanding the Reserve Army, to which the Canadian Corps belonged, was Hubert Gough. Gough was a driving, impatient type of man and in the ensuing days would force his men to attack before their plans were in place and before the deadly barbed-wire in front of the German trenches was cut. His pressure for an immediate offensive was the principal reason for the staggering losses suffered during the days ahead.

Right on the heels of the offensive against Courcelette came Phase IX of the Battle of the Somme, the Battle of Thiepval Ridge. On September 26th, the 1st Canadian Division assaulted the German trenches that spread across the valley west of Courcelette. The trenches, known as Zollern Graben and Hessian Trench, were connected to the German defences on strategic Thiepval Ridge, west of the Canadians. The Canadian attack was timed to coincide with a British offensive against Thiepval. East to west, the 14th (Royal Montreal Regiment), 15th (Toronto Highlanders), 5th (Saskatchewan) and 8th (Winnipeg Rifles - The Little Black Devils) Battalions successfully captured Zollern Graben and tried to push on to Hessian Trench, 600 metres to the north. A few of the attackers actually managed to reach Regina Trench, the third main German trench-line in the valley, 500 metres north of Hessian Trench, but were unable to hold. The fighting in Hessian Trench continued on the following day before the last Germans were subdued and the last counter-attack beaten off. By the time the Canadians completely overran the trenches, the incessant shelling had often reduced them to shallow ditches which could hardly offer the conquerors any protection.

In the meantime, the 2nd Division attacked out of Courcelette village. The 31st (Alberta) and 29th (British Columbia) Battalions probed northwards searching for German weak points, but achieved only limited success. However, the next day the Germans retreated to Regina Trench leaving the village cemetery and the important heights north of the village to the surprised Canadians.

The fighting in the trench works, west of Courcelette village, was continuous with no respite from death. The shelling never stopped and as the German artillery had all positions pinpointed, death could be sudden and at any moment. The fighting challenged the bravest of soldiers, but even courage was not enough to overcome the confusion, poor planning and uncut wire.

Regina Trench

R egina Trench was the longest trench constructed by the Germans on the Western Front. It was four kilometres long and it snaked along the valley of the Ancre River north of Courcelette. It was built taking advantage of every contour of the land and its principal stretches were constructed on the down side of the contours so that much of the trench was hidden from the Allied artillerymen. Like all the other main German trenches, it was well protected by formidable barbed-wire. It was only two kilometres from the Canadian jump-off line of September 15th. On that date, it was protected by three other key trenches: Fabeck Graben; Zollern Trench and Hessian Trench. By the end of September, the Canadians had captured all three at a cost of 15,000 killed, wounded and missing. They were now ready to take Regina.

The rain at the end of September created another adversary for the attackers. Autumn is always a rainy season in Northern France and the fall of 1916 was no different. But now, after months of continual shelling tearing up the ground, the battlefield conditions deteriorated badly. As a result, the unlucky troops encountered the "Somme" mud. It was a chalky grit, a heavy, sticky, paste that stuck like glue to the soldiers' equipment and uniforms. Some soldiers became so caked in thick mud that their uniforms and greatcoats weighed 50 kilograms.

The battle for Regina Trench epitomizes the futility and sacrifice that was the Canadian contribution to the Battle of the Somme. It took four attempts and a month and a half to take this one trench. Yet, it was only 600 metres from their new lines. And for what?

The First Attempt: October 1st, 1916

T he British High Command ordered the Canadians to capture Regina Trench at the end of September. It was to be an assault by five depleted battalions on the section of the trench north and west of Courcelette. Two battalions of the 3rd Division were to attack on the left and three battalions of the 2nd Division were to carry the main assault. Regardless of advice that the wire was not cut and in general the German defences were not reduced by artillery fire, the attack went in.

"Before the attack took place scouts had reported that the wire was very thick and that it appeared untouched by the artillery. Only one small gap existed on the left... Due to the position of Regina Trench the artillery had great difficulty finding the wire... The barrage which was supposed to have been laid down 100 yards in front of the enemy's trench had gone too far and the Germans without hindrance manned their parapets and wiped out practically the entire Company as it struggled to get through... However one officer and the remainder of the Company, found, as anticipated, the gap in the entanglements... and fought their way into Regina Trench and held it until the last man of them was killed."
                    Official History of the 4th Canadian Mounted Rifles.

On October 1st at 3:15 p.m., the 2nd Canadian Division made the first attempt to storm Regina Trench. But, the assault was too rushed and the attack deflated with only small groups of Canadians actually entering Regina Trench. They were mostly killed or captured. The 3rd Division's assault also failed for the same reasons and very quickly the Canadian offensive collapsed. There was one important success. The 25th Battalion captured Kenora Trench, a "switch trench," connecting to Regina Trench. From Kenora, an attack could be launched, under cover, right into Regina Trench. However, this was small consolation for more than 1,000 casualties and virtually no territorial gain.

The Second Attempt: October 8th, 1916

The Canadians' largest assault on Regina Trench came on October 8th. The attack was made by the 1st and 2nd Divisions and was launched over a three kilometre front from Destremont Farm to Kenora Trench. Eight battalions were involved; each Division supplied four. The 3rd Division's battalions, the 49th, Royal Canadian Regiment, 43rd and 58th, were to drive forwards on the left of the front, north and west of Courcelette. The 1st Division, the most successful of the Canadian Divisions, was ordered to overrun Regina Trench north and east of the village. As with the previous attempt to capture the strategic trench, the Canadians reported that the preliminary bombardment had failed to properly cut the maze of barbed-wire in front of the German positions. There were other ominous portends. Weather conditions had worsened and the thick mud which inhibited easy movement had become more of a problem. However, the warnings fell on deaf ears and, as before, the attack went through.

At 4:50 a.m., in total darkness, the assault was launched. On the left, the 3rd Division's battalions were stopped by the Germans or driven back by concentrated counter-attacks. Again, uncut wire had left the attackers stranded in No Man's Land and easy targets for the German machine-guns. Although isolated groups, particularly members of the RCR, managed to occupy sections of Regina Trench, they were forced to retire; many were killed or captured. The four attacking battalions of the 3rd Division suffered 941 killed, wounded and missing. Obviously, courage was not lacking; it was the same script with the same results.

On the right of the 3rd Division, the attack of the 13th (Black Watch of Montreal) had failed in the face of uncut barbed-wire. The men of the 16th (Canadian Scottish) also met wire that was intact and were stopped in their tracks. With the battalion pinned to the ground by machine-gun fire, one of

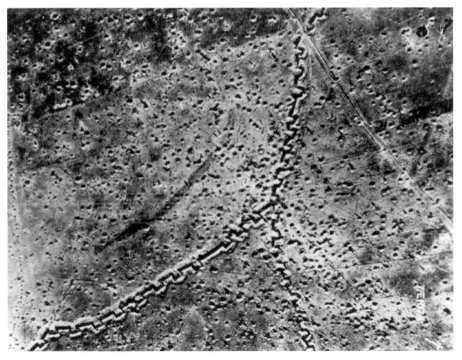

Junction of Regina and Kenora trenches: note the shell holes (PAC 14151)

the bravest individual acts of the war propelled the attackers forward. Piper James Richardson, seeing his comrades prostrate on the ground and their attack doomed, stood up and started playing his bagpipes. Seemingly impervious to the German rifles and machine-guns, he marched back and forth in front of the enemy wire. His example of remarkable bravery in the face of fire so encouraged his comrades that they leapt to their feet and stormed the German trench. The 16th Battalion had succeeded. They were in Regina Trench!

"On coming in sight of the wire I ran on ahead and was astonished to see it was not cut. I tried to locate a way through but could find no opening. When the company came up the enemy started throwing bombs and opened rifle fire. Seeing a big shell-hole on the left I ran over to Major Lynch to ask him to get in there until I could get the wire cutters to work on the wire, but as I got up to him he fell - shot in the breast. I knelt to bandage him but saw he was breathing his last. Piper Jimmy Richardson came over to me at this moment and asked if he could help, but I told him our company commander was gone... Things looked very bad and it was then that the piper asked if he would play his pipes - 'Wull I gie them wund (wind)?' was what he said. I told him to go ahead and as soon as he got them going I got what men I could together, we got through the wire and started cleaning up the trench."

W.D. Mackie, 16th (Canadian Scottish) Battalion.

The only true success came on the far right where the 3rd (Toronto) and 4th (Central Ontario) Battalions of the 1st Division broke into Regina Trench and the adjacent Quadrilateral near Le Sars village and then linked with the 16th Battalion on their left. There were now three Canadian battalions in Regina Trench, but they were practically isolated from the other assault battalions and from noon onwards were mercilessly counter-attacked by the Germans coming down the portion of the trench they still held. The outcome was inevitable; without support they retreated. By the morning of October 9th, all the Canadians were out of Regina Trench. Another ill-prepared attack had failed with disastrous consequences. The day's action had cost 1,364 casualties.

One of the dead was Piper James Richardson who had been killed while evacuating Regina Trench. His bravery was rewarded with a well-deserved Victoria Cross, posthumously. James Richardson was almost 21 years old.

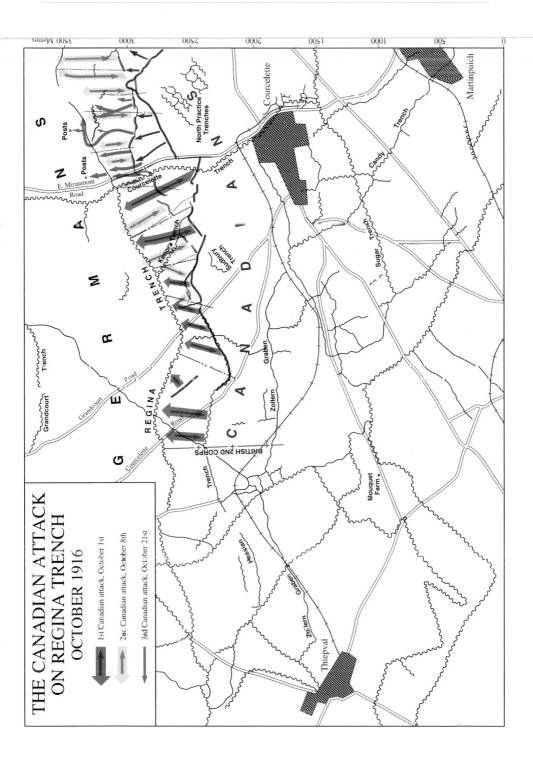

THE CANADIAN ATTACK
ON REGINA TRENCH
OCTOBER 1916

1st Canadian attack, October 1st

2nc Canadian attack, October 8th

3rd Canadian attack, October 21st

3500 Metres 3000 2500 2000 1500 1000 500 0

Martinpuich

Courcelette

North Practice Trenches

CANADIAN

Candy Trench

Trench

Sugar Trench

Graben

Zollern

Trench

Mouquet Farm

Hessian

Zollern

Gropen

Thiepval

BRITISH 2ND CORPS

REGINA

Courcelette Road

Grandcourt

Trench

GERMAN

E. Miraumont Road

Courcelette

Posts

Posts

Kenora Trench

Sudbury Trench

REGINA TRENCH

22nd

This was the last action of the Canadian Corps at the Somme. Exhausted, the three Divisions withdrew, tallying their losses at 20,000 killed, wounded and missing. The initial attacks on September 15th had been so promising, but in the 23 days that followed they failed to advance even one kilometre. In the process, they had learned many important lessons about effective planning, artillery preparation, and the threat of counter-attacks. Their courage had not failed them; their tactics had. They had mastered these lessons well and would apply them with unparalleled success at their next big battle when they achieved the impossible at Vimy Ridge.

The Third Attempt: October 21st, 1916

Although the Canadian Corps was leaving the Somme battle, the Somme had not seen the last of Canadian soldiers. The 4th Canadian Infantry Division had arrived in Belgium in August 1916. They had spent August and September learning their trade in the Ypres Salient. In mid-October, they made their way south to the Somme and came into the line opposite Regina Trench. The battlefield must have shocked the green soldiers who had yet to participate in a big attack. Their turn would come on October 21st, 1916; their objective was to secure a section of Regina Trench.

"I got my first glimpse of death and its stench at Pozieres. The dead had not been removed, and they were piled three deep. What an awful sight! ... Now we came to the trench. God forbid anyone from seeing what I saw. Our barbed wire was fairly well intact, but it hung full of dead Canadians and Germans, like birds on telephone wires. The parapet had been built up but you couldn't avoid the arms and legs that were sticking out of it."

Jim Broomhead, 46th (Saskatchewan) Battalion.

The 87th (Grenadier Guards of Montreal) and 102nd (North British Columbians) were assigned the task of capturing a 600 metre section of Regina Trench between the East Miraumont and Pys roads. This time the artillery had done its job and the troublesome barbed-wire had been cut. In a quick attack, the two battalions overran the trench. Within an hour, they had consolidated their position and placed "trench blocks" on both ends of the trench section, as the rest of Regina Trench was still in German hands.

Surprisingly, the success had cost a mere 200 men. Thinking the Germans were on the point of breaking, they launched another assault. On October 25th, the 44th Battalion (Winnipeg) drove against a portion of Regina Trench east of the Pys road, but the wire had not been cut and again, hasty planning resulted in 200 casualties for the new unit, and no gains.

"Huge shell holes, half-filled with water, pitted the fields in every direction... Far beyond Coucelette I saw the German flare-lights and the bursting of shells. It was a scene of vast desolation, weird beyond description... When I got into Regina Trench, I found it was impossible to pass along it, as one sank down so deeply into the heavy mud."

Frederick Scott, 1st Canadian Division.

The Fourth Attempt: November 11th, 1916

On November 11th, the 4th Division threw three battalions, the 102nd (North British Columbia), 47th (British Columbia) and the 46th (Saskatchewan), at the nearly-obliterated Regina Trench. The attack was preceded by two days of heavy artillery bombardment that smashed the defensive wire and offered the Canadians the opportunity for success. They rushed across No Man's Land in the moonlight and quickly captured Regina Trench. The Germans appeared to have had enough and offered little resistance. Regina Trench, after one and one-half months of battle and thousands of casualties, was finally in Canadian hands.

"I found Young about halfway over. A shell had caught him on the hip and had blown his right hip off. Of course he was dead. I knew he was from Ontario and was an only son. I would have to write his mother. We put him in a shell hole and covered him with some earth, but I noticed he had a signet ring which his mother would probably like to have. I tried to take it off his finger but it wouldn't come. My sergeant said, 'I'll do it for you.' So he took out his clasp knife and cut the little finger off my pal and gave me the ring. I later wrote to his mother and enclosed the ring."

John Copp, 46th (Saskatchewan) Battalion.

The 4th Division was not finished on the Somme. Pushing northwards, on November 18th they launched another small attack with five battalions totalling about 4,000 men. They rapidly captured Desire Trench, a trench

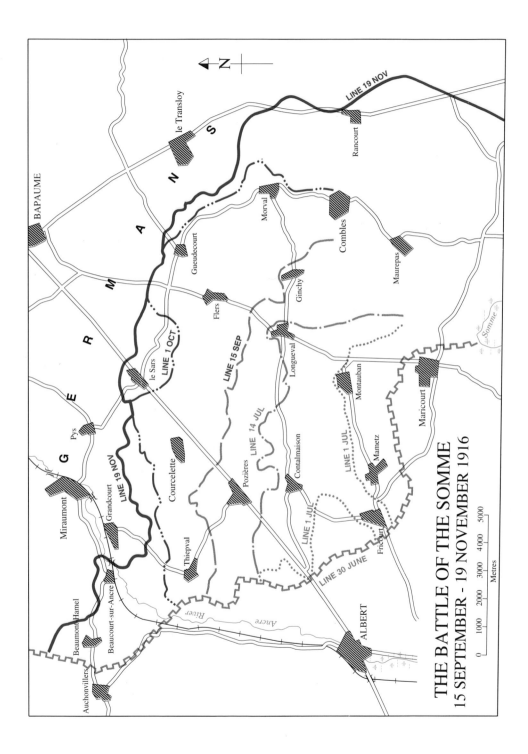

THE BATTLE OF THE SOMME
15 SEPTEMBER - 19 NOVEMBER 1916

600 metres further north of the obliterated Regina Trench, and managed to probe a further 600 metres north before being forced to return to Desire Trench. This last action on the Somme cost 1,250 men. The 4th Division was relieved at the end of November and joined the other three Canadian Infantry Divisions in the Canadian Corps in front of Vimy Ridge.

The Battle on the Somme ended on November 18th, 1916. One of the bloodiest battles in the history of warfare was finally over.

The Aftermath

Why had the Battle of the Somme been fought? For what had more than 1,200,000 men been killed or wounded? For what had the cream of a generation died? Most military historians agree that there was no strategic value in capturing the Somme or even defending it. More than anything else, it was a battle of attrition which, numerically speaking, the Germans could not afford to wage. It also bled the British forces badly as the Canadians were to experience first-hand. They fought and died, like everyone else, with bravery and courage. But, what had Canadian valour achieved?

"Lice, rats, barbed wire, fleas, shells, bombs, underground caves, corpses, blood, liquor, mice, cats, artillery, filth, bullets, mortars, fire, steel: that is what war is. It is the work of the devil."

Otto Dix, German Army.

Tactically, the Canadians had learned to appreciate the importance of careful planning and artillery preparation. The perfect execution of the Vimy attack in 1917 came from the failures on the Somme. They had witnessed the birth of the tank and before the war was over they would use this weapon more effectively than had been dreamed of on the Somme. They learned a personal lesson too. Never again would the Canadians serve under the impetuous General Gough. At Passchendaele in 1917, the Canadians were placed under him, but they refused to accept his command. Surprisingly, the British High Command allowed the Canadians this unusual request. No doubt it saved many lives in the mud of Passchendaele.

But all of this would be little consolation to the families of the more than 8,000 dead Canadians. How could they justify the loss of their loved ones for the gain of two and one-half kilometres of mutilated, chalky Somme farmland?

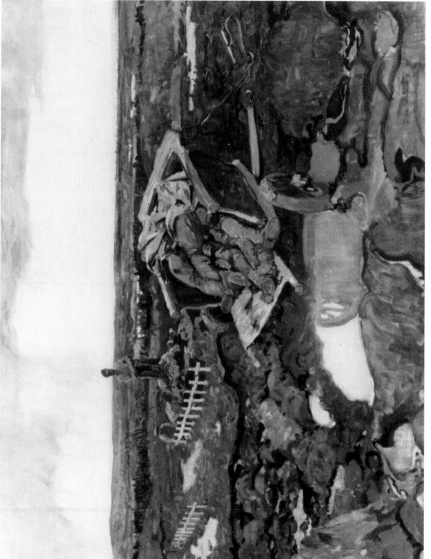

For What? by F. H. Varley (CWM 8911)

The Odds

A shocking statistic of the Great War was the tremendous loss incurred within a few hours of an attack being launched. Suffering 60% to 70% casualties was typical for an attacking battalion of 650 men. Of every five, one would die and two would be wounded.

Of the 370,000 Canadians who served on the Western Front during the Great War, 60,000 died. This represents a startling one in six. However, the 370,000 is not a true reflection of the dangers of front-line fighting. It includes men who never served in France or Flanders and men in low-risk units such as the Army Service Corps, the Cavalry, the Siege Artillery, Lines of Communication, Railways and Forestry who rarely came under enemy fire.

For an average soldier serving in a front-line battalion, such as the Canadian Scottish 16th Battalion, the chance of being killed was one in four. Two out of four were wounded, and only one in four came through the war unscathed.

Overall, the odds of dying of wounds were one in ten, but a soldier's chances of survival depended on the location of the wound. The number of Canadian soldiers wounded in World War I was 144,506. Most of the wounds resulted from exploding shells.

In many battles, such as Passchendaele, difficult and dangerous conditions prevented removal of the wounded, who often succumbed to their wounds before they could be given proper medical attention. In the later battles of 1918, the medical arrangements and transport system worked like a well-oiled machine. At the Battle of Cambrai, for example, the wounded were evacuated from the battlefield to hospitals in Rouen and Boulogne within 24 hours.

The toll of the wounded is sad reading:

Types of Wounds

Head and neck	22,284
Chest	3,780
Abdomen	1,395
Pelvis	53
Upper Extremities	51,508
Lower Extremities	43,652

Suffered ill effects of gas	11,356
Wounded who remained on duty	7,602
Wounded accidentally	2,247
Wounds self-inflicted	729

An unknown Canadian soldier and his mother in Montreal prior to going overseas. Once he left the shores of Canada, his chances of being killed were 1 in 7; on reaching France 1 in 6; and on reaching the front-line 1 in 4.

Execution by Firing Squad

M ore than 350 British Empire soldiers were executed during the Great War. Twenty-five of these men were Canadian soldiers, all of whom were volunteers. Twenty-two were executed for desertion, one for cowardice and two for murder. By contrast, the Australians did not execute a single man during World War I.

Military authorities deemed that certain offenses, considered minor in peace time, could not be tolerated on active service. For example, desertion, which normally resulted in a two-year sentence, could bring the death penalty in wartime.

In theory, each man would receive a fair trial with assistance from an experienced defence counsel. The judgment would be based on the man's record and fighting ability, the extenuating circumstances and previous convictions. Desertion to avoid a major attack and any prevalence towards desertion in the soldier's unit were also considered during the deliberations. In situations such as these, it was argued that an example had to be made to prevent similar behaviour in the future. If found guilty, the man's sentence would require approval by the chain of command with final authorization coming from the Commander in Chief.

The procedures for the execution were well laid out. The soldier's unit was responsible for carrying out the sentence and the convicted man could be attended by a chaplain, if desired. The soldier would be identified by a noncommissioned officer of his unit before proceeding to the execution site. A stretcher would be provided if the convicted man could not walk.

A Firing Party of one officer, one sergeant and 10 soldiers would wait with their backs turned to the execution post. The prisoner would be brought to the place of execution, blindfolded and tied to the post or tree. The Medical Officer would fix a small paper disk over his heart.

The Firing Party would turn with five men standing and five men kneeling. One of the Firing Party's rifles (unknown) contained a blank. With the command, "Fire", the deed was done. The Medical Officer would inspect the man and pronounce him dead or, if still alive (which did occur), the officer in charge of the Firing Party would complete the sentence. The body would be removed for burial and the correct paperwork completed. A volunteer had died for his country.

For official purposes, the man would appear on the casualty lists as "died". If his next-of-kin asked for the particulars of the death, the officials would contact the clergy in the man's hometown. If the clergy believed the family, due to age or state of health, could not cope with the truth, they would not be informed. Secrecy also helped the next-of-kin keep their social standing in the community. It is unknown how many families of the 25 Canadians executed were not informed of their son's or husband's execution.

Of the 25 Canadian soldiers executed, nine were from Arthur Currie's 1st Division, eight from the 2nd Division, two from Louis Lipsett's 3rd Division and three from David Watson's 4th Division. Statistics apparently suggest more compassion for their men from the Commanders of the 3rd and 4th Divisions. The other three soldiers belonged to the Artillery, Cavalry and Army Service Corps. Four of the 25 were not tried by the Canadians, but by the British. In these cases, the Canadian Expeditionary Force was notified after the sentence was passed.

By battalion, five men of the 22nd Battalion (Canadien-Francais) and two men of the 3rd Battalion (Toronto Regiment) were executed. No other units had more than one executed. This statistic seems to illustrate a bias against the French Canadians for, in addition, two French Canadians serving with other units were executed. The disproportional number of French Canadians executed possibly represents more than poor discipline in a fighting unit.

Political motivations may have played an important role in the death sentence given and duly carried out on Private Demetro Sinicky of the 52nd Battalion (New Ontario). Sinicky was tried and convicted of cowardice in the face of the enemy. He had no previous convictions. His commanding officer presented no report and no record of recommendations regarding the carrying out of the death penalty.

Sinicky was Russian-born. After the Russian Revolution of 1917, paranoiac fear spread through the Allied armies concerning the rise of Bolshevism. A mutiny of Russian troops occurred in France. The Canadian Corps reacted by transferring many Russian-born soldiers from front-line units to the Railway Troops. Considering Sinicky's record, something else must have determined the death penalty.

Three Canadians were executed for desertion during the Battle of the Somme. Their trials are summarized as follows. Judge for yourself.

PRIVATE HENRY KERR: 7TH CANADIAN BATTALION
TRIED NOVEMBER 7TH, 1916, FOR DESERTING HIS MAJESTY'S SERVICE

"The accused absented himself from the support trenches, after having been warned for the front line, and remained absent till found in billets, some miles in rear, twenty-four hours later, thereby avoiding a dangerous duty.

"The reports rendered by his platoon commander, his company commander and his commanding officer on this man's conduct were extremely bad. On one occasion in the trenches only on threat of being immediately shot would he leave his dugout to carry out his duties. So bad, indeed, was his example under shell fire that his comrades on the last occasion in the trenches at which accused was present had asked that he might be left behind in future. It was also stated that he continually threatened to shoot officers and NCOs.

"All authorities concurred in recommending the carrying out of the death penalty."

Shot November 11th, 1916.

PRIVATE ELSWORTH YOUNG: 25TH CANADIAN BATTALION
TRIED OCTOBER 19TH, 1916, FOR DESERTING HIS MAJESTY'S SERVICE

"Accused was an officer's servant. On 16th September 1916 he was returned to duty. His company being in the line, he was ordered to report to his Company Sergeant Major, who was then at Sausage Valley on way up to the line. (Heavy fighting was then in progress on the Somme). He did not do so. On 29th September he was arrested by the Military Police at Abbeville, a good many miles to the rear, disguised as a corporal of the Artillery and after having given false details about himself.

"Conduct sheet contained five entries, all relating to minor offences. There is no record of the recommendation and report which is made by the Commanding Officer in all death penalty cases but in his evidence before the Court his CO said the accused had been with the battalion since 1914 and though he had been thoughtless and careless and was undependable nothing had previously been brought against him regarding his conduct in the line. Brigade Commander's recommendation in this case is also missing. Divisional Commander recommended commutation of sentence.

Corps and Army Commanders disagreed on ground that offence was deliberate, in order to evade fighting and C-In-C confirmed."

Shot October 29th, 1916. Aged 19.

PRIVATE JOHN HIGGINS: 1ST CANADIAN BATTALION
TRIED NOVEMBER 26TH, 1916, FOR DESERTING HIS MAJESTY'S SERVICE

"The accused left his platoon without orders when it was proceeding to the trenches during the fighting on the Somme and remained absent till apprehended by the French police behind the fighting area sixteen days later. After his arrest he escaped and remained absent till again apprehended five days later.

"Accused only had one trivial entry in his conduct sheet. His conduct up to the commission of the offence, both from a fighting point of view and from a point of behaviour, was reported by his commanding officer to have been satisfactory. Nevertheless, as the offence was deliberately committed to evade duty in the trenches his commanding officer and all higher authorities considered the sentence should stand."

Shot December 7th, 1916. Aged 24.

Bibliography - suggested reading

The Somme by A. H. Farrar-Hockley: B. T. Batsford Ltd., 1966.

The First Day on the Somme by M. Middlebrook: Allan Lane, 1971.

The Official History of the Canadian Expeditionary Force, 1914-1919 by G.W.L. Nicholson: The Queen's Printer, 1962.

Somme by Lyn Macdonald: Michael Joseph Ltd., 1983.

The Canadians on the Somme, September - November 1916 by N. Christie: CEF Books, 1996.

Ghosts Have Warm Hands by Will R. Bird: CEF Books 1997.

Letters of Agar Adamson edited by N. M. Christie: CEF Books 1997.

The Journal of Private Fraser edited by R. H. Roy: CEF Books 1998.